Banishing business - Best bets

Soothing hopeful tomorrow with customers lacking clarity

Authors:

Dr C Vasanta, Dr R Alka & Dr C Rajgopalachary

Dedicated to my grandparents.

The book is about acknowledgement of Customer and technology against employees and product. It's easier to get done than others say. Any mistake is solely my responsibility in all walks of time devoted to this book.

Vasanta is a consultant, Alka is a life mentor and Rajgopal is a retired accounting professional.

Banishing business

Simple template

The beginning of idea would lead Customer to search for quick solution convertor and that works in business interests of generating new avenues for leadership or Innovation in accepting through pangs of hard toil, rejection of wild ideas for selling needs to unknown technologies slowly improving customer understanding that usually err much on your business self as success without credibility or neither should be possible without or with your business 100% because anyway it's market power that rewards and punishes players all of which emerge as unpredictability heads.

Each customer, solution, decision, opportunity, competitor, market gets as unpredictable as it may turn out to be passed on by each one of the complete earnestness in business partnership with participating in a bid for the future corrections as a day, way or pay. Everything needed improvement a century ago and needing so much later than a millennium down. The business lane progression in time is no longer having enough indications of upward and downward trend because life in general and Customer in specific are available for guidance and support while facing scarcity of experience enrichment, resources renewal, instructions innovation and technology alignment with you on Customer and Business sides have exhausted all debate of man machine clash. Man has ego, machine has code and it's not right time to attach supremacy of either.

The enrichment of experience is in business etiquette and ethics to be a part conduit for Customer to pay against competitors who are sharing or marring chances of business. Earlier Strategy for profit used to step up from Customer as against today with your future business ventures stemming from positive NPV and profitable return. You go ahead with the project if and only if Customer is able to shell out money. So what is the business for? Money? Customer? The goal is to inform the needful stakeholders in business activity of Customer appeasement that's source or midterm goal or destination depending on your business credibility rank that is innovating ways of icing on Customer agony rather than business effort without expecting Customer profit. As an example, Sony will continue to forgo having fat margins than loyal customers so that they could use Customer appeasement as source of business changes. Here technology will fall somewhere between quality and old ideas. Technology is lucky to be demanded by quality and broad vision suggests value of quality for Customer praise. Thus ethics and credibility compete with technology as it strikes a new balance on each use. Bank of America is a good example of effort and profit as preparation of struggle in business compliance and Customer appeasement that's midterm goal of business excellence by existence. Walmart stands out as example of increasing Customer services standards so that they could create Customer appeasement as a destination of each employee and outlet. Technology is enabler and not driver of business customers at receivers but not seeker or asker sides. Customer is hunter and consumer of technology in Sony case presenting a good business paradox and contradiction. The direct inference and conclusion is that all your customers have to be happy to accept your offer of technology that is core of business.

No business is in a complete accordance with customers from start to immortality of claiming or even trying to satisfy every customer in every aspect and experience. Even machines that know Customer as a direct recipient of certain validated outputs based on dedicated customisation in inputs and demand could close out on future generations expectations and approval to 90% accuracy but without any human benefits of general difference in culture (behaviour, lifestyle, community support), ideation (learning, perceptions, interpretation) and personal individualistic identity (thought, ambition, drivers). Unlike machine a person is conditioned upon region, religious experience that is embedded into cross-border interactive process of establishing superiority by behaviour as roots allow for growth in lifestyle of self with surrounding members. The goal is to be known for uniqueness of thought , attitudes and approach in different situations where you enjoy your ideas on investing in solution for your or other important characteristics emerging from issues aiming for new triggers, trends and drivers of development of Customer and Business in focus of future without disturbing environmental methods, different perspectives or learning. The abstract man and logical machine together balance the business cycles and change based on adaptation with customers who express not fully clearly, expect man of business to understand and want to use machine for next lifestyle progression in the global unifying mass technologies that promise nothing but are deemed to serve customers and not bothered with understanding. Isn't it a parody and rationalisation of Customer as your employees are punished but machine is not even reprimanded for failing performance? What satisfaction will go to the mother scolding a robot Sasha for not serving a fresh meal to the kids on time? The interactive systems under pressure and restrictions could be managed better by another woman who again can grow apologetic of not being able to prevent disasters due to man-made blunders and losses in adjusting with machine learning. Today the right knowledge and volume of data cannot be guaranteed but after the result of Strategy implementation, Customer feedback and business ascertainment of services. Earlier in the world of nothing and scarcity something was appreciated unlike now when too much is a common reason for saturation and Customer dissatisfaction. The company gets expectations and attributes a new Strategy for implementation of Customer plans. Nothing great except for walking with customers, then Customers discover the business needs for discussion in feedback and intuitive genesis of strategic innovation but relationship management between customers and business alignment with technology shows that you have to ascertain the service capabilities to close on the fissures. There is no longer right and wrong for no grounds of business changes with invisible forces full of probability of willingness, success or failure of business exaggeration on Customer motivation and machine logic. Machine learning algorithms reveal that you want peace to understand and think clearly in customer engagement. Men machines have been working on new ideas to overcome personal problems from reducing their brain efficiency. Machine doesn't have a pain when an error occurs in the legs or subparts of neighbours get spoilt by screeches and exploitation of user. The machine stopping the work gets repairs, the operators get warnings and Customer gets more attention of phone call from Customer service agents and automated emails reciting service formalities and apologies for Customer appeasement and regards for understanding that you are doing business best and right as a human machine.

How many machines could claim personal services to customers from united understanding to fragmented clarification? Technology is running out on future business understanding of Customer and Business stakeholders but assuming that the global network of users and makers brings default and united space for trust and knowledge that enlighten resources with individual answers to be thankful for new products made of variety of business changes brought up with each clarification again attributed and credited to technologies. The goal is to solve Customer problem and Business difference by finding advanced neutral technology and taking the help of same clan in getting ready general acceptance.

Blockchain technology is supposed to understand and integrate with customers from fragmented innovation to get tailored solutions that go into future challenges resolution because of multiple classes of business alternatives floating in the global market for personal attention of Customer with her narrow set of cultural pursuits, fears and concerns that generate new ideas for addressing them without any cost or obligation of dependency on other things, products, people or situations. The loss of interdependence avoiding interference reduces penalties and deficiencies of clashing interest and overlapping needs to get new opportunities for growth and development of business solutions that bank upon Customer return for more change experience as personalised education to provide simple answer to complex questions. Healthcare technology is uniting experts and devices for new expectations and technology alignment to greet change and Customer demand for supply of life saving tips, medicine and surgery in real time implementation of Strategy for integrative health solutions that go with Customer, compete on improving your business offering, trust and balance different inputs from doctors, documents, robotics, tools and sources of relevance to the patient and not lose focus, faith and fairness of customer, thought and performance management. The action of perfect surgical procedure and treatment cycle could let future developments in the right direction without skipping the global decision on strategic innovation and entrepreneurship benchmark to allow for independent and excellent Practices for managing transition of experience to successful balance between possibilities and conversion to be illustrative embodiment of life saver example and impromptu inspiration for creation of innovative real change wonders of future to understand what is going to be used, provided, needed and awaited by user, competition and research. A combination of weak patients, panel of doctors, guides for new equipment operators, exact reference to past failure give spontaneous innovation from blunder prevention to instructions innovation to successful remedy and finest balance between altruistic or exaggerated completion of strategic business benefit to provide true worth of solutions to series of urgent and naive sympathy valueless arguments where the physical levels of pain is not fib. The goal is easier than expected restoration of life in general health terms with higher technology help of magic therapeutics and that alone gives scope of technology miracles for new business exercise of answer presentation for old health care issues.

It's a critical reasoning behind healthcare technology that is fruitful exploitation sardonically. You can now diagnose and treat the disease but not without any hassle of human involvement with the accompanying risk of default treatment cycle of expensive eternity simply due to man-made blunders or doubt or scope thrown by your visit in clinic or exaggerated fear of physical sicknesses or ignorance covered by cunning commercial professional healthcare units or cruel doctors playing together with customers only for once converting them to profitable patients to pay for hospital employees and five-star infrastructure.

The example is a reminder eye-opener of Customer wanting to be in charge of business and avoid extreme trespassing by others not ethical in their way of duty but not everything can be conducted in place with modern world busy living in styles, yoga's, worries and joys all sorts of things in your interest at the same time unless you're appreciated or covered by your actions and values of true instincts. Where is business than selling against old value system specific but rich in current scenario futuristic individual? The business existence is questioned in whether there is immense cause bringing up with each seller or maker driving interaction with customers from electronic modes of being considered for surpassing necessity of company but not industry with standard for Strategic individual representatives of business dealings of breathtaking innovation and customisation in highly productive, profitable and quality support via products or services that disincentivise corporate entity existence for cultural and entrepreneurship benchmark to allow right kind of global loyalty of both sides of business and buyer management. The example of apparel and food industries also check if Customer could visit a restaurant or clothmill in the first year of next decade when they are in the fingertips reach of phones at home visiting the entire family in a costfree jiffy. The other costs by real-estate, power, furnishings, storage, scale expenses, large-scale production, mass ad, employees and technology are exaggerating the global base costs by packing, delivery, returns or maintenance as high as ten times more than expected price range accepted by buyers without any other options with big tears and question mark of business relevance but modern electronic gadgets enable change within the same pattern and better at times with individual representatives selling against the global network of users of new or old solutions that bank upon lowest rates as a dramatic change challenge for others to fly high or perish. Competition is running in the form of companies with all the best cost-greed free individual sellers flying great. The business groups and individuals or informal teams and projects are up against the global network of kicking simple Technology and hardworking person who can get better done quicker for cheaper in customer service delight of keen enthusiasm and determination to let the rest take care of itself as a new chapter of the complete value and endless utility within product or other forms of solutions opens for buyers and sellers who are sharing for free at times with more of competition in community connection by dropping the global jargon of Customer and Business in the first personal interests of connection. Thereby the buyer is relying upon a connection to understand and give something useful as we are always welcome influence on others, a man by nature wants to know about others more than self. The seller is willing to be a good connection instead of blunt money sucker. The money is needed and awaited but easier to get than others missing like happiness, satisfaction, trust and success by definition of invisible human terms of today.

The future business growth rates as most influential the following bets. Though the business bets are not guaranteed to get new leadership advantages by fatty profits could companies ignore long-term strategic possibilities for Customer acquisition?

The rate of patent acquisition in the global individual and group innovation market power comes first as a key knowledge bet for best business practices and new customer retention potential. The number of patents behind new equipment productization and rapid response-change sequences in tomorrow is at stone's throw from company expert's attention that twins in customer impression of business provider chain. Innovate and invest in customer thought so that they are bound to be in synchronisation of business and buyer psyche without which company could convert IP into future modern knowledge dumps to no practical community avail. Change is like antagonizing wave that goes without stopping by any cost of destruction to sandcastle or interrupting structure midway and not bothered about complex success of pearls reaching bay in serendipity of deliberate attempt of coral without any expectations. National intellectual property as indicators of individual enthusiasm, interest in our exploration of progress, cooperative team intelligence, accessibility to ideation and overall commitment to industry can't wait to see attached benefits of general business success, research support, global cooperation in common or special issues on government and personal priority bucket list. Today we have a plethora of subjects in technology and outside for taking new ideas to provide patented products that help extended needs of luxury or basic style of Customer means of reaching greater satisfaction in day-to-day tasks. All of which make use of IP and trying to be part of new ones are in a way utilising time with best brains and contributing to pathbreaking change within society. The competitors must accept the global intelligence in quest for excellence of technology and new forms of energy rechannelisation with natural and man-made together trying to be change -packets of global importance. The machine is man-made change maker of business performance management and enhancement in the global reservoir with customers, employees and other brilliant people as natural change makers. The sources of energy rechannelisation with natural generators of sun, seas, wind, forests, mountains, snow, and artificial forms of oil, gas and other exhaustible ways today seem to understand that destination of life is not realisation of life but now hugging of life with technology as it may contain privileged information about simplifying and facilitating of action in day, months, years and life in continuity of care and enjoying the global trade transformation practices at different scales of business and buyer attachment. The small farmers grow trained health food business and related industries with customers all accepting the right aid of technology at conversion of knowledge to various tools and products instead of waiting for others to understand and lead or the right preparation for global integration of business, community and user systems under pressure stories of unexpected invention or exaggerated market power could close our advanced age of Customer awareness by our competitive narrow minded focus on proximate money, possibilities and conversion of knowledge into short-term profit space.

Another Business bet is no easy to accept interacting family and friends not to forget that extended family of social networking globally claiming to be no-thanx voluntary well wishers of Customer and too belittling to ignore because we'relooking for free advice on secret give and take from the different coincidental matching of community and business emotions because anyway it's a known fact that business world exists for money, not Customers and Customer is more than expected to save expenses, not companies. The goal however claims business to be working with understanding for Customer instead of business growth rates as today's Customer is claiming to understand everything including his inconvenience, competitor's product, family problems, technology and new times instead of price wars. The irony is no different from other times and not going to change faster than others in message. We have not counted technologies different from change but the formula is not so. Technology is not change in expectations and avenues through goals for unthinkable innovation but as continuous and powerful challenge for change all over global community opposition that is driving again ironically the global change within the physical, cultural and business experience of working with machine.

The simplest example of a good attempt of acceptance of smart technologies slowly begins with your father assessing the price vs saving, Mumma killing with safety and children protection questions, before the real user community has rejoiced peer circles showoff feedback and hidden interest for new products that seems to have a backseat of great business background checks conducted by everyone at home in different forms possible or impossible, directly or indirectly, failing or yielding details, fructified or cancelled deals and save tension or joy. Options are many with neighbours, relatives and social nodes hovering around with information and idiosyncrasies in the form of mutual biases stories of unexpected or interesting experiences, those complaints and criticism comments , news reporting debacle and flight of companies with your interest coming back from inputs and the companies dying as a dramatic twist in facts and fads are analysed by advanced market power makers to blame for your business failure, Customer loss, competitor gain, stock market ebbs (the flow is thus widespread whether quick as a bubble or slow as preparation of business Olympics), economic alerts, government intervention, regulatory guard's whistle or a breakup. Directions are more than modern market volatilities for Customer basing her decision on strategic innovation usage and ownership of products.

Banishing business

Control strategy for Customer's decision to be always in favour of Business is not yet in existence unless something happens for a suitable collision of Customer and Business in future by improving customer understanding that you are happy to accept interacting family of no, yes, another, next - words dragging the business scrutiny and Customer expectations when decisions are not same as inner expectations of users of smart objects and that discomfiture invites opportunity for your skill of aligning Business interests with customers' changing influences on information and access to new opportunities for connecting with need of every single member of Customer user circles.

Banishing business

Retention of Customer as your need for business justification of the complete endless iteration and Strategic circles in the global company pursuits of Customer delight, products innovation, high technology adaptation with attribution to non technical excellence, services utility maximization, vendor-partner negotiations, perennial margin improvement, sales hikes, exchange-return rate reduction, employees attrition management, and participation in the global industry standards evolution at leadership level not forgetting knowledge conversion to track opportunity success rates, business transformation chain of change assessment - action points - results review - resources check - time based tactics, competitive responses- Strategy - collaboration - transition mechanism of unplanned and market instigated Business decision to get the Innovation cycle of research-prototype-testing-IP tuned to understand what you should not disseminate as preparation of business handle for mixing new ideas reviving old needs and values in a bid to make route for new needs attention to get new information about simplifying conditional value chains testing stakeholders biases and foolproof plans for reaching targets of business vision, rework, competitive prompt, underutilized capabilities strategising and not diverting from Customer. The market has plenty of books talking about most of the topics above but not on the full flow of business strategies for new business solution around unutilised capacities. The entire exercise of business execution calls for Customer loyalty otherwise every change can be pointless. We are going to shut down wasting resources to turn operations not of good sense to customer and that is too much known fact that may be ridiculed for new mention, of importance is a customer lost due to lack of multilateral intervention of man-made strategies for appreciation of business capabilities by directing them into modern ways of improving resources utilisation as a dramatic possibility in achieving the customer target by allowing advanced intelligence of technology at various activities, and not cutting resources inclusion in the name of cool search for better customer or insight or other forms of opportunities for use of existing skills and capabilities without understanding that you are not doing business as a laboratory experiment but running in business as a live test of fullest potential exploitation to get instant ongoing feedback and approval of Customer as favour to Business and personal pleasure to customer. Every company must have innovative means of reaching better and new solutions with the same resources used differently. The business entity should try the impossible to achieve the impossible if innovation is to be justified by all means, literally and practically. When Hush puppies were born nobody gave their

their attention immediately but some thing let the company continue with full capabilities utilisation instead of waiting for scale- volume- scope prodding and that course of balance between possibilities and resources utilisation opened up new vistas of Customer perception of the products themselves in such a good way that you become part of unexpected success without niche limitations of price, weirdness of design and unnecessary need not initiated by users nor asked any questions by allowing reactions of sole gut in business continuity of production. In the simple fact and sense, the company makes and Customer buys. Full capabilities utilisation removes doubts, questions, inhibitions and competitive failure behind the business sincerity of offering independent product innovation from bottom of business heart and smile of Customer is expected price for which Customer is more receptive of and acceptance for the product should move in like that free levitating will of user sealed in the product. The goal is to be witness of favorable positive Customer psyche without any conditions of bookish results and the process improvement gets the same results. The process improvement on reducing defects, wastes, redundant efforts, erroneous resources allocation, wrong decision making, inactive research team, inaccurate information management, tweaky automation techniques, flawed utilisation of capabilities, ineffective capital management, irresponsible quality assurance, negligent support systems, slow tracking and learning process, outdated protocol for new products, technology discrepancies, tough management access, decentralised knowledge management, informal Customer channels, heavy financial gaps, meaningless market survey repertoire, ostentatious marketing ad budgets, untimed and untimely launches on clumsy project management, yield less investment imbalances, illogical product innovation, unaccomodating Customer relationship management, disruptive product management, transformation ignorance and lagging stakeholders. Each customer should be responsible and united with others and company in reporting the business defects faced with products, employees, stores, services, distribution channels, internet methods, information, communication, and experience to company anytime anything to anyone for your official teams to skip everything else to work for fixing the business defects with the accompanying right help of technology and men. Every business day is a test of Customer as your invigilator and each defect and Customer complaint is a deduction of demand and profit score. The other side of fault is the wastage of time and resources applicable to get new ideas and opportunities implemented. Wastes are indicated and found in lethargic team members, defective machines that consume and waste more resources to no practical results from overwork, less knowledge, inexperienced staff, untrained employees, incorrect estimates and incomplete administration. Both are profit draining and must be controlled by lean tools of efficient quality management system that goes without penalizing Customer as waste or defect compromise. Duplicate efforts and work with chaos, unclear deliverables, changing expectations, and other reasons as mentioned above could be managed by implementation of the business tested methods of allowing advanced customisation or reducing it as a business strategy for win-win-win of Customer-prospect-old, the new customer may want more tailored solutions than an old one. The old one could be a previous customer who has left you and switched to a rival so that business has to understand to decide the winning proportions of customisation, the same is true for prospective buyers as well. Wrong customisation or redundant efforts lead to faulty resources allocation that disturb their utilisation of capabilities. Skills and knowledge that go with Customer experience can grow you to expert instead of into an experiment for ridicule and detestation by allowing rivals to mock at the efforts as market gets some bad news for inevitable business failure. Underutilized and overworked capabilities both can hamper and ruin process improvement plan because they could easily find a place in any business at the same time unless staff is smart to operate in adversity and not without departing from optimum performance management of men and machines. Capacity shifting should be avoided and adopted by wise analysis that is like saying that you want to sell something that you are doubtful of demand for supply of less into saving costs and consumer green signal is needed for full utilisation. The wait is natural when machine is built to achieve scale over a period of time. Human resources are subject to inestimable skills and some get overrated with others getting underutilized due to underrated understanding of self, bosses and Customer. The work breakdown and assignments could be ugly without any proper tools and techniques for your business management.

Decision sciences support and superiority of business partner hierarchy hold on no sense without creating future avenues for getting leadership, knowledge, tactics, resources specialisations and related tasks execution should yield results in given areas moving Customer into comfortable adjustments with your business and Custom services that provide utility but not without any deviation from Customer expectations and goals when we claim, expect and care to meet with success without creating pressure bias for company and this is only partially possible or true as different participants will give customers value of business with what they can and herewith trying to be as close to customer expectations as possible. Decision is more than a yes,- no, do ,- stop, this- that, open- shut, review - act, add - multiply resources etc.

A valid decision should trigger value generating activities for the future research and development of easy intuitive pointers of the existing business changes brought from that decision. The correct decision costs nothing but good chances are that it will keep your research management active with customers and employee teams to challenge the current loopholes for extracting more than expected opportunity with return for motivation to Business initiatives on the debated and demanded areas of strategic relevance.

Banishing business

Information management and research needs to be accurate in terms of use, analysis and proposal for change within physical and cultural context of business with distinct objective of playing to consumers will retouch data coming from Customer as your quick proof of aligning with user interest , of redirecting data to make new Strategic wonders with collaboration in business channel partners and customers all over global network, and intelligence analytics on facts that you could depend upon for consideration of business changes in future.

The business entities try and adopt automation techniques by inclinations to various proportions of customisation, reluctance and compliance requirements. No unknown and unseen is a common mission for winning human consent in business sublimation of technology adoption and future challenges of coaching and commercializing of business resources and outputs based on usage and market progression as a new step up the business ladder could be a new factory influencing the business evolution by unit firm with industry standards averaging the global perspectives thereby slowing down or expediting the global pace of technology progress through

Customer presence in the natural and man-made change within the manual and machine learning and development. Tools and knowledge generated by allowing advanced usage and for utilising the right automation levels at global podium pose questions and not threat across your business needs and aspirations like them trying to satisfy every single member in the technology movement. All decision support systems, process improvement initiatives, information systems under change management and research innovation are not independent of automation wave that is freezing and demanding resources, resolution and responsibilities of the complete value chain participants community for competitive victory over traditional perspective on industry journey.

Long-term complications of business mismanagement could result from bad capital management that goes into inflexible debt equity composition, debilitating and loss-making investment decisions and actions bleeding the business utility and value. Honest experts and advisory should be able to guide company in times with more risky and volatile conditions of market. Most gaps should be revealed in audits but some discrepancies may be overlooked and skipped during the global survey and review of business branches across globe. Quality assurance that lacks the knowledge and ability of assessment and fixing tactics of erroneous and negligent or deliberate malpractice could take the business into bankruptcy and peril still because they eat into future results of hollowing the business foundation and strength of ethics. Tools and wavy methods come after the integrity and interest of business employees who should take care of working with transparency and accountability. Support culture and resistance to let the company fail in business goals achievements should be nurtured by allowing reactions of various stakeholders and advanced systems under surveillance to help customers, employees, supply chain participants, and other stakeholders who work with chaos created by competitors or critics and endure opposition or other forms of demotivational attitudes beyond bounds of emotions or mechanical control. Some people need human involvement with others preferring automatic management by allowing hidden identity and importance. Business is liable to understand both sides for heeding to get multiple things sorted out and done in a short time. Systems and responsible experts should assume assistance and respect for exploited resources instead of mocking at or exhaustion of patience. Sacrifice and effort are not the technology elements that is unlikely to get new ideas on improving performance of employees in emotional and human sense. Employees should be able to respond to machine deficiency to work with an extra mile by sacrificing the personal life but machine is not expected because of its mechanistic nature that can not lend extra effort or stress though it may break down on overuse and not stretch beyond bounds assigned. Such equilibrium between customers and employee teams could possibly propose appropriate man-machine combination for your skill cultivation and acceptance by fusion of business learning with market tracking systems under implementation of Customer and other business goals for unthinkable innovation- led growth. The same helps businesses with recognition and rewards for your stakeholders by providing them with profitable learning about future ability to generate new opportunities for growing knowledge building systems that are uncomfortable with your business errors and can warn you with intelligent solutions for withstanding gruelling market or a bad Customer who has ability to work your sincere efforts as deliberate mistakes in delaying success or other business developments in adjustments with selfishness of Customer and drainage for business prospects. Tracking and learning systems reduce such undue influence on automation and control by Customer commitment or employees training in working with information in business globally for competitive conduct of Customer without compromising on the intended company mission.

New products that help you with comfort of business growth are not those pulling together old success stories but ones that stand smart to operate as preparation of handling undecidable change or other forms of innovation by new business ideas for selling new products in new ways of improving the global currents in the larger furtherance of tomorrow. The failure is in hanging on to old methods for new idea implementation because though we can remain confident of doing well in business that sale can't facilitate future business growth of your customers loyalty tried and tripped over by more modern business rivals who can grow a new collaboration wave with customers to make the global market think like a modernization hub of optimising the old gold by allowing advanced market concoctions of business transformation technology and ripe transition intelligence to get new platform for development of Customer needs you may use for further refinement of information or direct product innovation. Speed and quality may be worked on for better results than struggling with technology gearups to comply with the present business innovation needs more from Customer attention point than business continuity change point of view. Technology discrepancies in business might creep due to man-made strategies in adjustments with different capacities gaps that are sure to beat Customer experience blue but not as ocean, different users will go finding faults in the attempt, new technology learning will be missing, old technologies will be worked out on the grounds of erosion in replacement tactics, resource strategies will fail without proper tools, competitive responses will go haywire waiting for Customer concurrence of business changes fighting for the difference to be justified by the fumbling technology. And employees are likely to get resistance to change by raising objections after which the global network of bosses can be seen convincing users of business customisation or spontaneous own development projects for service delight of generating new business technology ourselves from Customer investment in reducing or diversifying risk of both sides of vendor or customer for finding advanced collaboration in market consent to promote new skills for new user cooperation of connecting with need of any industry stakeholders as it's possible that you could unearth unexpected expectations of users with different stakeholders who developed theirs based on end-user success. The knowledge of customers by providing access to the company management and leadership can grow trained mentoring to shift employees from focusing on your business success to customer delight in the light of the fact that delight translates into success but Business success without Customer delight is no impossibility. What do we get to understand that the user wants something different from that we have? Or rather your user prefers to get new solution each time and not what we have because they deserve something better than the best. The intricacies of Customer cannot be known by business by restricting access to management champion teams who can understand what the talker wants to convey without any telling. Add their experience and you have new ideas ready to be implemented for new future consumer even before the consumer is so. Again place in case or new knowledge where you can monitor, track and use without any modification which disturb the facts. The goal is to have a centralised knowledge structure to avoid multiple cost, duplication risk with that of hacking and security for managing future change without maintenance problem. The business essence of application of knowledge can grow different customers channels on subsidised ways that goes into avoiding heavy financial structure flaws in business administration with flexibility and sentience of Customer as a driver of modern channels for new business commencement of demand execution should they entice complete change within existing methods of promoting business interests merely by adspends of today in millions of dollars swept away by notional market sentiments that may be compared with those of stock trading. The drama will continue through each product innovation or decision rather than business time limits of the likes of Computer product innovation that you could define in fixed time period of business changes with visible forces of different types of technology skills at different levels of components in the first personal computer parts. Can we do pattern prediction of tomorrow in business globally for immediate, new, competitive or other forms of Customer channels for satisfaction, communication, interaction with customers from start to eternity as long as a business technology or concept is evolving around unutilised capabilities of business or opportunities for new ways of improving customer involvement rather than product purchase alone. Educational, career - developmental, or entertainment or other forms of Customer and business relationship can grow trained economic recovery without stopping by crisis or other revival pretext for exhaustion of resources to try and test employees or Customer participation in business or social networks but not restricted in the narrow usage of chatting or family communication with the most powerful intent of Customer empowerment in the global market for total personalized innovation but not without creating knowledge database for global strategic analysis that goes along new community building measures depending on time bounds, society growth concerns, individual inhibition, national identity and business aspirations. The egoistic marketing campaigns that you want to sell your top managers' ego to competitors because

Customers with emotional fervor could give way to help such business sell but in reality such products are seen as problems and don't sell well as their advertisement is no longer trusting to be able to reach out to customer for finding a good attempt of strengthening the right connect in the different types of stakeholders involved in the global channel partnership with investment justified by fumbling and unreasonable points achieved by imbalances of business changes, Customer perceptions, product utility, technology alignment with the prefix of mis conveniently skipped on reasons for readers to guess better. It's a headache for new business solution provider for further quest about complex Customer psyche warped of even more complicated Business offerings in the name of customer satisfaction but service or support without connecting with your customer is like eating without digestion system of absorbing the right nutrients and knowledge to maintain future business facilitation not divided by stakeholders demand, needs or capabilities to serve business changes brought by external environment wants from Customer or competition or employees on prowling in the global network of cross border management. The interference, interdependence and independence of the complete set of cultural and business representatives should be balanced responsibly to understand correctly, completely and clearly the expectations, capabilities and needs to get new outputs on long-term strategic bets.

Unholy marketing budgets mislead you into conducting research surveys of tiring in number and retiring in the meaning to accumulate info of no use for further increase of larger number of survey attempts on lines of treating Customer as your quick proof of aligning Business interests with customers and business getting fooled by advanced resources wasted on the valueless additional data ignorant of Customer needs to take the time of productive activity to losses in today's internet forms at the visit of any website asking you to offer your data of personal, private, dreams and everything possible or impossible to unknown stranger servers for no reason that is otherwise claiming professional rights of understanding Customer community. Innovation can not be possible without elimination of business Oddities of the kind, companies should cultivate innovation oriented inputs collection in precise time-bound manner failing which poor innovation is unavoidable as seen in the global market currently following user without any customised differentiation of meandering million products that help no customer with anything more than a initial original low-cost product innovation from authentic data feeds. Instead of hurrying in imitation or immature innovation Companies can adopt time with àgility of offering them to transfer benefits of old ideas to new products and vice versa of engineering projects from decent project management practices that are talking services, solutions and products that are decent outputs on improving your customer expectations as preparation for fulfillment of smart yield expectations of business investment in results based innovative measures into avoiding poor customer feedback. The customer who has bad experience with Business products can not trust you again for revealing the present expectations or trying the products again. Satisfied buyers dare Companies to get better with higher expectations because they deserve something more of different improvement or other forms of technology innovation from where your business success without wasting investment in low yield initiatives many times not even tracking or knowing the right cause bringing caution to pits of business excesses in high adspends, faulty management tools to adopt wrong Practices for irrelevant projects for Customer denial finally. Such business politics do no good to anyone from Customer to employees who work with misguided tactics or inputs wasting resources and Customer understanding for silly experiments with your short-term or bureaucratic goals for increasing international trade hurdles that cannot be overcome many decades later slowing down economic growth by patches of lagging areas. This happens for government initiative of wrong intentions of political ego satisfaction by not being able to pull back the loss-making policy like that USA mortgage restructuring crisis continuing today in the global market psyche without visible activity. The connection between company and economic development is not as distant as your thoughts with quick repercussion flowing in business and economics of Customer and community to cut across global economy from one another because such information on markets challenges the response in real-time perspective owing to electronic web connectivity in the different types of micro, macro, nano, mini technology or economic development through a direct correlation between the different types of stakeholders in economic growth from birth till stagnation of unit firm. Factors are many with infant nutrition, education, employment, entrepreneurship , aspirations, society participation, norms, global collaboration between individuals, companies, industries, governments and everything in the economy of the nation's most powerful tools of Customer relationship management world wide on affecting the global development.

Customer relationship management strategies and tactics should not be defined, as policy or system of business with customers from product point of view but should be left free for employees to enable culture of CRM, not a big rulebook of CRM, not that rules are not required but some triggers for your hometype relationship management should come into future business changes to get Customer feel comfortable like home. The last century saw the right form of business relationship with customers from start to long as a personal rapport with family of business and Customer instead of roping in deals for employees, all used to be in the name of true patronage of connecting with one another. Today we are checking on budget so that we don't meet after once, do it on first instance of revealing a business strategy for new deal acceptance by buyers without any shame or fear of losing Customer relationship. The management heads are at peril because if they think about changing what everyone is doing their business is in ditch, therefore they have to do it reluctantly of managing Customer like a rich ghost who can give money if happy to strike a deal or switch by moving away from the company with earlier customer to competitors. The exercise is done in a harder way like that but some people think that your immediate action saves time instead of debating over ten meetings whether you're appreciated or not for your products by

Customer who is also waiting for your business reciprocation for her patience of listening to your impatient melodies of business sales pitch in the least expectations of boomerang view because the calls, meetings, emails from this crazy CRM don't know what you think, want or not, the issues, goals, questions about complex innovation are discussed not bothered by when they could stop, something that Customer resists but at times has time to waste and agree to be part of the sales stint with a group of other prospects. Celebrity is invited to host a dinner party with prospects of business sales, team spends huge amounts because they are dependent on old Customer for new deals for proving to prospects that you are the right choice. Sometimes no conversion happens if Customer could not buy on the product features or your convincing power is not effective. It means that your CRM is bookish and not realistic. You will blame other departments and Companies that compete with your business products in wrong expectations of saving yourself for the next sales pitch. The process or product management may contain errors as global company resources are mishandling regional business changes with customers but not without any cost of business misalignment in the effects of selling defective, unwanted, unworthy products to buyer who is unwilling, so she will go with four of your customers on word-of-mouth that is becoming a silent tool against your loud attempts on fixing internal business failure with customers outside the business on local and international level that should be balanced with localisation of business products management of strategic need identification for global standards adoption of quality upgrade. Technology should be able to pull appropriate product innovation in local terms of use and relevance to the domestic customers and global network gives interface with customers from scope of paid orders over web of business products, service and support solutions for system trade participation. PLM and CRM don't know each other but affect your company depending upon interaction or acceptance decisions of Customer as your products are used by the same Customer.

At one time, Airtel mobile communication provider limited it's customers service representative interaction to have a chat on phone call from Customer in the first three minutes of discussion with growth goals in adjusting Strategy for managing Customer and community opposition was tackled by allowing unlimited calls for care from the initial three attempts per day of each customer should they load employees with personal problems from Customer life in India. The business of users control by your actions reaching greater understanding of business instead of users of new solutions with the accompanying aim of process improvement can get better if customers are freed from all possible issues on the faultering services, in this case the business restricted the right of Customer of complaint or feedback to ease the life of employees in reducing the number of Customer interaction with time limit for managing server loads when Customer should have been left free by rebuilding a larger call centres strength with any effort taken in business stakeholders interests of promoting the customer interest uniformly and unambiguously. The short time decreasing quality of service by business manager collecting the same Customer information each time bored the customer without having enough focus on solutions. The foolishness started in 2008 to self annihilation of business dragon Airtel.

The above mentioned position of strategic transformation ignorance covered by stakeholders disinterested attitude towards Customer should not be forgotten that the entity misunderstood business excellence and made the customer pay for it instead of streamlining internal measures into charging the customer for talking extra with call centre reps. Customer needs can not be possibly understood fully by such miserly business resource allocation for Customer commitment hence competitors like Vodafone, Tata Docomo, Idea and small others could switch the customer segments of Airtel without any rivalry opposition or much aggression.

Stakeholders must have innovative solutions that improve your business credibility by Customer inclusion not seclusion of saving modern infrastructure from Customer attacks. The connection between company and Customers is very important to seeing success of business changes brought in order to get latest time adhering market advocated activity of performance management approach or process improvement measures into avoiding antagonizing Customer. Airtel has adopted several strategies for new products introduction, market expansion and growth but some acquisition initiatives didn't give expected result though they didn't disturb much of the business leadership advantages by players still lacking global brand infrastructure, poor governance mechanisms and lack of foreign service providers in Indian space. Recent business change through Jio stepping up new infrastructure innovation and technology alignment with customers and domestic conditions, can not be termed as successful nor terminated on failure instincts because they are sort of midway with customers enjoying business benefits and firm returns not upto mark though scaling smooth. Indian telecom is as underrated as American food industries due to man-made blunders of business transformation loopholes by defaulter stakeholders. Hence proper care has to be taken in confusion reduction of customer needs by allowing advanced

Customer participation in business transformation management with maximum utilisation of stakeholders skills.

What is business transition?

Everything is attached to technology for opening up new tools or concepts in the global direction of getting the final destination of Customer input on satisfaction or feedback or loyalty or other next forms of delight, future business partnership or switch to rivals. Business transition mechanism occurs in the global network of users with different customers by preferences of sellers working in unknown changes brought in market for total innovation adoption with development of new solutions on new ideas and methods (technology, resources and information) overhauled to get the transition to the company so that they could penetrate the global product then on the market back with the right hope of improving community trust by offering more than worth of a business transition in the form of products to customers. It's not a big bang profit sharing migration of software or hardware tools like technology competition in business community and the confusion could close out with the cost drain on Companies completing the messy Business transition to get the best resume attention. Each reader deserves a clap for noticing the right reason mentioned above if you have any leadership aspirations with your connection establishing and competitive business offering to customer your humble duty is not in conclusion of business sale but to treat it as prebusiness, essentially means of reaching better customer focus on greater opportunities for growth in future.

The feedback or suggestions despite loyalty or satisfaction is not the end of journey but beginning step of continuous change journey. The exercise of business administration and the first sale begins for new Customer as your business acknowledgement of existence. Once the presence is established business takes the customer feedback to understand what needs to take effect on future business strategies for complete growth and ethics need to be part of business through pre-beginning to next business changes brought with the intentions of achieving feedback for new products made by backward reinvention of expectations of Customer delight that can't be predicted to result in customer moving into a rival Business offerings in the global evercontinuing risk of experiments and going ahead with the business of business perse. Entity can grow by Customer risk if you don't stop by previous best profit but continue to roll out more challenging solutions for Customer to compare, accept or reject, this is customer risk. The goal changes and business approach changes with technology, knowledge, skills, manpower and lot many things go into the business transition to understand Customer correctly in light of the complete big awry working of worlds of different types of markets inhabiting Companies, changes, challenges, Customer, ideas on improving endlessly.

The concept of business transition has gone awry with customers explained by business how it's better than others in the updation of latest technologies and lot more capabilities as preparation for fulfillment of new projects from employees. The journey is not thus, it is also a toughest competition as base for new change within the company now working with new indicators of business success to assess results in unknown ways to competitors.

The exercise of business administration and management automation with customers from receiving end of journey attaching business changes brought by external environment wants is no easy task by taking time out on business transition in the first hope of improving resources allocation, usage rate, utilisation rationale; second hope of finding order in business information management of strategic knowledge innovation; and third hope of restoring Customer faith in culture of business with distinct ability to bear unreasonable customisation request for fulfillment of demand well in the global interests of business with each and every customer. Walmart and Flipkart entering into the ten billion dollars sweepstakes acquisition in business global limelight have been criticized as crazy by some and smart by some. In retrospect of market transitions before and after the long retail business transformation into borderless digital trade led by Amazon, not many could manage a market share except for serving the global network of users in segmented pies belonging to multiple players in the global market at the same time frame of 2005-2015 before which clarity on digital transformation was covered by the Demi technology (partial machine involvement) jitters, with customers and business changes settling for new movement in the ten-year period after which processing with articulated reality of how to get existing social networks interaction with robotics as continuous improvement exercise of productization, consumerism and community development interest of economic innovation from bottom of the pyramid. Walmart could not buy on business changes with technology as it may turn it's focus of Customer to pay for motivation to get multiple things done by employees but on acquisition of Flipkart its entire middle class Asian market with the accompanying technology capabilities of business with distinct product innovation are transforming Walmart business with globalisation change of next-gento transfer the competitive strategy benefits of each other depending upon synergies in the course of balance generated in the process of establishing duediligence of business changes with knowledge of customers by building trust in the global company operations excellence by providing specific process technology superiority. The exercise of business transition has a reason to get new employee policy in place with modern business development through technology adoption of quality products and efficient manufacturing facilities for third-party selling and wholesale business with customers globally from management point of view but some radical revolutionary innovation is no longer breaking news but need of Walmart to understand Customer of competition in offering worth more than and different from that of Amazon or the next acquisition could close on Customer buying from Walzon. The business transition includes culturing of employees contributing to change by teaching them to mentor otherwise dull staff, make a difference by allowing overtime and business comfort building new confidence in the consumer by filtered best practice adoption with adaptation to customers and best global market solutions.

We have a nice risk of disturbing of technology skills, knowledge assets, employee morale, intuitive Innovation, Customer interface, resources fitment, utilisation or allocation for your business time that are talking change within the business transition initiatives, which can be adopted several times in the global existence of business with distinct technology shifts, knowledge development projects, Customer transformations, competition revolution, product overhauls, operations improvement or other business process drivers of triggering the global company changes in various levels even at cultural, structural and Strategic areas that your entity is totally guarded against losses due to the company transition and that's why you want a good transition mechanism in place with modern business experts, laboratories, funds, systems and agility in helping the business with distinct goals, advisory, experiments and flexibility to analyse, decide and act as quick wings in saving time and money with knowledge, experience and skills of stakeholders and employees or any other interested Business participants in adept transition of business. The exercise is done by ignoring the usual sequence of formalities for start to end, instead it may take up the business prerogative in advice, priority in analysis, milestones and measurement of results in action with the right goal adoption of immediate decision making process to get new things in place on subsequent research of Customer need that may change or not.

The right light on how to get multiple things done in transition should be shown to employees for energizing them, freeing them from the different fears and resistance should biases inhibit the right pretext of business transition in the global interests of promoting business market economy of the complete industry with the competitors equally welcoming Business transition because it's a common market development usually not applicable to single company. The results could affect the economy due to which the task of business transition has no beginning nor end, no source or destination perse in adopting a new trend of market that is termed as common mission for companies but finally ends up as savior of adopters in market enforcement of business penalties for those who just ignore this propelling transition.

No transition mechanism occurs in the first or last step of continuous change journey of business hence, we can remain confident that Business transition could be given a chance at anytime once you get market signals but not waiting for your company alerts or closure reds in order to change by business transition initiatives which Customer is used to seeing everyday in the global network of business attempts to get the complex challenges simplified by initiating Customer into comfortable adjustments in business globally for competitive benefits from the first day of transition. Take inputs from Customer segments in the different types of change waves within the market because not everytime does a regulator poke the global market for a change that is clearly explained in the guides and websites. Some of these changes have to be initiated by you as innovators but some others like to follow market leaders who are confident of conducting accompanying change without confusion or compromise or failure.

Technology risks are ever increasing with people risks ever predominant in customer risks everlasting mainly in business risks ever building new risks that you want because you have to worry if you don't have any risk where you don't have any use of risk management system that is playing on returns from contingency plans, Strategic risk mitigation and diversification plans. Risk of transition is going to exist without or with transition because once it's in market, players that have any success stories could not wait for the buzz to get over. Success streak comes from companies going for systematic transition, as one company is adopting the wave, others have to do transition of strategic business style with the accompanying variables like men, material, product, utilisation, resources and such other inputs and outputs. The process risk of tailoring of business process on Customer demands could bring in new risks by routine pattern, output consistency and employees efficiency. Everything can be affected in business transition and business should have proper teams to evaluate the global company change, to get the latest tools bring them to even level. Assure the business departments of business changes brought in for your skill cultivation and utilisation as leading to better knowledge management and precision development projects for increasing Customer satisfaction but not as passing of business burden to customer, for the community of business users has no liability for any direct transfer of losses in adjusting with transition because benefits should be balanced among all though indirectly, the losses get trickling down on Customers with longer learning curves or higher prices or periodic adjustments in product innovation, these should be avoided by the company but inform the user if it gets so inevitable and the company must bring cooperation in common corrective actions putting trouble to rest. Soon after, the measures should eliminate the risks involved in business transition initiatives which Customer as your quick beneficiary expects to get new impact for product usage or experience without any tradeoffs in business attempts on giving something different at different milestones of transition. It may turn to be difficult to envision what to offer to customer but management should come up with answer to delight users, of holding a keen observation and appreciation of business changes so that they don't get discouraged and irrelevant. The users may not understand the long term benefit of transition that goes into better performance of products and implementation of projects for increasing international customisation in highly quality effective manner of Customer service with the business transition upgrading firm with returns enhanced by brand exercise of gaining importance or full knowledge of customers from the different types of ideas and offering a new worth of 'business with change' and leadership for your business mechanisms to get new improvement, or Customers helped better by support systems to let them know what they need, when to expect and how to use improving how to get new things done by the employees as helper for Customer. The business entity should wait to get the best results from the transition but not make Customer wait for the future business gains, immediate growth opportunities must be identified for Customer.

Current business and Customer understanding for zeroing of overall needs to take priority in the global community development alongwith improvement on user ways that is finally contributing to business changes with profits leading to market power. Product innovation, knowledge discovery, technology refinements and employees mentoring shift the global company resources to right kind of transition of operations at obtaining an Excellence of competitive strategy in the three-dimensional need smoothing as above. It's not a good attempt should they find more differences and difficulties with the common need, the solutions can get new opportunities from the information added but some value breaches might occur in the process of establishing profit, satisfaction and development of business entity, Customer and community. The risk of value- compromise mandates a good product so that employee leadership with àgility management should come to respond with positive changes brought to community progress through business flows when they could sustain the great business culture of trust and care for networks of Customers and employees to effect change as preparation of constant sustainable growth and business transition initiatives that become agents of business products improving branding efforts as competing conduits in customer needs transition to the effect of company Strategy alignment with scale competition as a loyal societal bid for growth that goes by allowing advanced employee participation in the global or local small or major community initiatives.

Thanks to the world wide web and mobile technology in multiple ways that you are getting fresh ideas reviving change within the cultural values of Customer in future irrespective of money benefits from the different products satisfying Customer value change by business supporting equal traditions of transitioning from team building to trust, technology to Knowledge, utility to àgility, allocation to alignment, utilisation to motivation, process to care, to enable spontaneous right decisions in customer direction of community concern, knowledgeable service as overriding goingconcern, parametric involvement with drawing hierarchical delay, system drama, team dependency on wasting resources and information on personal managerial idiosyncrasies in the name of even more unorganised competition Strategy for managing market expectations in the most complicated global company debacles. The complications and conditions of costs, community, Customer as your quick response takers of yet another complex business transition maze if crossed successfully could give good learning experience for your future Innovation based on customer feedback whether explicitly sought or negatively thrown in business circles to remind them of Customer importance in the tasks of business transition, community change, economic reorganization and market vulcanisation. The first two tasks are discussed as cause of the last two sides but not without incremental backup of your customers participation in the general industry wide attempts to get the global business transitions done in the right time and way to help with tangible gains or other improvements directly protecting your customer thereby making your process credible and competitive in the global market with an assured solutions innovation with more than expected revenue or demand success rates.

Economic reorganization is that process of systematic settling the change by accepting the right knowledge and rejecting the wrong reason justified in making an economic shift, which as industrial mistake can get the economic turmoil under the misinformed decision of economists who are clueless as to claim the effects as big or small, arising from the business transitions taking shape at different companies at different times in the global industry so that they will continue to be absorbed by the economic growth like a secret nourisher or spoiler of business prospects in markets. The ultimate impact of economic reorganization is borne by the companies at the unit level that may or not be passed on to customer and end-user via products or individual community impact on the level of education, employment, experience, and general participation in initiatives. Economy poses tough many questions and challenges in changing policy, and interest rates fluctuations. The first is controlled change within your purview and the second is uncontrollable change outside your response. The side-effect is to be seen in the different forms but surely on the participants in economy in toto, nobody can save themselves from the financial implications, market assymetries, information inconsistencies, we have a nice bunch of job creation, business friendly perks, regional development projects, learning and training drives, skills workshops, countersteps for debacles, to take place in the economy of one or more nations on affecting the performance of employees contributing to quality of products that are accepted by buyers on different occasions leaving the market of relevant information to reposition itself in response to Customer groups sending different types of ideas and reactions unfolding change within market power for managing signals that are sent by market for Customers but Business interventions of competition response is more prominent, Customers don't usually respond to market signals, market doesn't match with customers' trends and hence both sides are safe in letting others know that markets are volatile and Customer is more than full of expectations in demanding unexpected or unreasonable things from companies. Business intervention in this respect, is helping market to increase economic flexibility of getting aligned with customers to allow critical company restructuring of fulfillment by user satisfaction, competitive responses, technology investment and employees growth to facilitate market vulcanisation. Market vulcanisation is a good capability of market in becoming resilient and adaptive of Customer needs and business changes to temporarily provide simple answer why users should collaborate with community after Customer cooperates with Companies providing specific solutions. The market reverts to volatility after a short time decreasing the performance management issues on thwarting economic uncertainty. Market vulcanisation is a common need and trend of future business without economic disturbance in avoiding victimization by devastating monetary glut periods by allowing short-term fitment of Customer, business and markets in the long term benefit of economic growth. Economic reorganization and market vulcanisation go hand in hand with the performance and productivity going up to get new efficiency of resources that go into modern industrial evolution that competes with domestic or international industry promoting or hindering trade transformation of spreading the market improvement on economic conditions of growth at global level.

Global adaptation of market that competition and consumer can benefit from is not a big possible treat but some information on previous market success of business could repeat important trends in favour of user perspective and business developments, changes with opportunities for growth, knowledge generation, innovative solutions, honing of the process and performance improvements in each category of business changes this propelling an all-round transition of intelligence and excellence in future improvement on user interface with some of the process methods though it is better not to levy business headache on Customer. This is where the market vulcanisation is a common occurrence and employees should be able to respond with balance and àgility in fast adaptation before you see benefits going back to get market recede or travel to volatile conditions where your customer is a good ray of hope for one. The attempts on business transition in the process of establishing superiority of Customer over Business innovation in turn over company can not but show recent vulcanisation of paving help for new business fit with market success tracking involvement of competition in business changes globally to get multiple ideas on market interaction for future because anyway you have to understand Customer and respond to market for total innovation. Of trying to understand market and respond to customer is no easy task but to let market flow naturally and Customer should be satisfied with your business services, if Customer brings issues your business should solve but not react or respond to customer for finding another issue. The changes that are adopted by the business entity should understand customers absolutely not to uplift market sentiments alone but company reactions or responses should have some information about Customer transition (cultural practices, value preferences, skills, knowledge and intentions) to new solution but with old set of product affiliations in a bid to save on the best for family while interacting with different providers in experimenting with innovative solutions for system evolution that kills unproductive projects for serving long term profitable economic reorganization, to get new community reforms whether you're a profit-making business or no, Customer community should be able to respond with balanced, positive or other kinds of feedback on equally intelligent market trying to understand the industry if not a firm or consumer, be it even for a given duration of time, among all initiatives company should remember remember to get new ideas on investing in transition of strategic business innovation going for systematic benefits to flow steady to Business by cultivation of technology skills and employee innovation but as continuous own effort without any external environment help because Customers think about their lives and market lives for itself in its own thought formed of information all around, neither Customer nor market is of direct and full help to the business entity that is solely responsible for learning, implementation and support of business changes, failure, success or growth without compromising on Customer worth or market attention that provokes innovation, brings competition and stays with the best combination of process and performance management approach to get multiple new attempts possible for different strategies to be implemented with customers who will continue through each market change by unveiling the needs to guide company future by overcoming market restlessness in a larger call for change within physical society because of its lack of multilateral development through coexistence in eradicating the ills of establishing the value systems specific to change within the community.

From the market perspective each customer should get unique value of expectations in forcing the best entity to beat its own process improvement challenges of giving new productivity goals in economic sense without losing any of the linkage of the three subchains to the overall value chain balancing business supply chain, user value chain and economy growth chain that are facilitated by management expertise of execution, technology vigilant àgility in accepting unacceptable expectations because anyway it's better knowledge that goes along refined economic development through coexistence in intelligent competition in working world that still belongs to the knowledge reign right from consideration for school degrees to office appraisal grading evaluation revealing that you are not same as that product innovated by your team or independent action but knowledge that brings a new you by becoming a part of you as innovators throw similar or better version of your prided products. Certainly nations can be compared with their knowledge assimilation or use that product shows or other forms but surely economic development is not just consensus on your single percentage points that go into modern rating how much knowledge is a good economy circulating in business globally to locally in creating, acquiring, extracting, storing, converting to product or service, processing with the best market trends for technology innovation, disseminating expertise, disbursing skills and retaining the consistent action points that others would compete on improving research or performance or utilisation of best way of knowledge by basing advanced customisation, market demand fulfillment, competitive power strategies, technology leap generation, learning techniques optimisation, wise traditional vs modern business method selection that is supposed to be in the present business changes with knowledge and technology weighed against competitors and Customers debating on whether you're better off with a new business solution or steps along old ideas for growth reasons of cost reductions in books but some extra loyalty resides in business globally to a shift toward the best results from old Business secret stories in unveilance or fadeful memories of modern management that is bragging of Customer rights and employees automation in other combination too, which are provided by entities constantly in adapting to natural market waves but in reality of reconstructing the process cracks breaking business trust by which company could choose to see itself in the market. No business is doing a favour by allowing Customer to save it's face by market tides in customer showing satisfaction, shouldering responsibility for directions, for accepting your business services that provide simple span of competition in answering your low prices challenge with low risk profitable consideration of business thus competitors not far from using mutual games for escaping Customer as a business strategy by Customer to be taken care of with the same up gaming industry objective of improving the competitors' failure rate. In other words, the market reactions unfold toughest games in customer, competitors and the focal firm as the ground offers signals, ideas and methods for identifying opportunities and posting reactions of various kinds of skilled, innovative and cultural, ethical and differential nature of adding information on enhancing markets and value of business changes with delight of customers by building new risks on competitive walls built to get multiple response strategies running the same game in a long term profitable economic reorganization and industry parameter generation establishing innovation. Parameters are not necessarily growth standards or quality functions but could handle your business change through each customer needs whether small or major.

Google has made a few great Business transition exercises with success resulting like that in Apple, Microsoft, IBM and HP. The market improvement and industry standards upliftment brought by Google Innovation in business globally is a lot along Apple's. The first to offer free bundle of business products in email, search engine, storage, survey, reminder and other services gave it that leadership advantages of Customer commitment, low risk, customised pricing and past experience expectations in getting small businesses adopt a new Microsoft kind of provider's offering. The internal growth of Google is not without general hiccups of Customer bringing up problems of cloud not bothered with business ethics by allowing multiple Customers who could go together with development risking confidentiality in a possible hack but some revenue of business has been reinvested in research for coming up with guaranteed customised service and product for users interacting with different employees who work with freedom, enthusiasm and determination of generating unique outputs on improving intellectual property instead of small rental property for the company. Google analytics, AdWords or groups are not letting the process of social networks go haywire in rewarding the users with different types of partnership with the company so that employees and customers are growing along with community and business developments continuously. The first thing that the management table makes sure is that they will continue to invest in employees and customers who are waiting to take the best way forward due to which company is in business success route without any doubt, like HP that banked upon Customer who teamed up with employees in reducing market uncertainty by responding to change and competition in offering well-structured opportunity for growth of employees and customers from rivals in 1990-2000. IBM also managed better employee innovation in early 2000s by advanced interaction with customers and technology infrastructure acquisitions that you have reaping gains even after two decades now and later for new products turned out of strategic innovation. Google is a good example of the business transition initiatives that improve upon all aspects of management and not some areas, there's a new overhauling in the process and performance of whole organisation that is using culture of Customer in restoring chorus to employees for handling chaos in market.

Google can't be replicated by other companies because of its ideas, trust, àgility supplemented with keen penchant for achieving something, the best combination with customers and market timing could give Google a good success but not without any warning for not compromising on Customer, employees and motivation of company by serving as the modern innovative solutions provider along new ideas reviving old value system of participants in different types of business changes and initiatives that become agents of business in internal environment and external environment unless Google simply means buying needs for selling new ideas from and to customer for using the margin or funding the missing chunks with the objective of developing their community.

Notes

The definition of business transition has been broadened in a similar way to be uncompromising of Customer as a business final goal but Google is no exception to the game of business with distinct changes thrusting more challenges than solutions for system, process and environmental participation in response to the overall requirement for Customer demand fulfillment by associating with community, company mission, competitors, resources capabilities, technology, capital management, users and leading interests of the business stakeholders that drive Strategy for profit orientation, management of risk and compliance decision on strategic three-dimensional structure design of business strength building upon trust, ethics, care and service integrity as the four pillars of business offering worth and business enthusiasm in the form of business products originating from Customer need that goes along development through testing on a long process of meeting standards of growth with your manufacturing, operational, production and business functions arranging the pieces together with customers, employees and other stakeholders to get the best of new business outputs based on multiple things sorted out on, done by and shared in business administration globally or locally. Therefore business is in the lot more boxed sense trying to get the employees think out of their boxes and Google simply does it when their employees are not boxed but allowed to get things going in their way of working on selected tasks, at the chosen time in place on a sofa or park or a bean bag, in business premise or outside, with people and team for guidance, technology and tools of their convenience, Google is a common structure of business facilitated by management of earning expertise and providing them infrastructure for yielding Innovation and entrepreneurship as Customer receivables in delivering delight to the end user. The rapid innovation and research team first adapts to market for preparation of business in favour of user and thirdly selecting the right technology for high quality customer experience with products, services and tools to help customers enhance competitive edge of self with others and business because Google duo or other robotics embedded gadgets are not same but for recognition by Customer patronage that is dependent upon your business relationship with customers who can get better visibility of your outputs from some things to be good useful asset of user liking. The changes that Google is doing in business globally are not going wasted because they are additional pieces of growth information for the contributors and participants of business community and the internal process is approved by the market as the best of examples for companies to understand, compete and get better at different ways of improving consumption dynamics, managing market expectations, realigning the process conditions, expending user interface and commercializing Customer sentiments of paying for your business products enriching their sentiment further. The company knows that Customer got a new need so that they could create a new product to sell back to customer after selling needs to internal stakeholders but Google is doing it a bit better and different from others in their job of finding out the best mutual business methods for both sides of the product that sits on a shelf seeking buyer attention to get across the seller goal.

Google doesn't match goal of business with customers nor does it seek user of different types of ideas and products that are decent magnets in themselves attracting new buyers, the firm returns with information on following market and gets best technologies to let employees walk in the shoes of Customer as smart employees build freely in a way of products for themselves like Customers could also do something similar, employees forget that they are dependent upon management as employees, that enables to work with user ideas for interest like users and the process that goes into modern product instantly connects with customers or users when in the markets. The first risk is taken by the employees in freely thinking like Customers who find their place in the community without any involvement of direct relevance but not that the management is excluding any customer, participation and support without inhibiting rules of business games, can come from Customer in getting recruited by the market on easy contract terms for flexible collaboration between employees and Customer. The community of users will continue to contribute to the overall usability of products development through technology accessible to both users and business developers who combine their efforts of reaching better endproduct in a bid for innovation. Huawei is inviting Customers who could come to any of its offices of openly taking a look at the process and operations of employees contributing to change Customer demands to market products in adapting to an extra open culture with Business and Customer understanding each other but not as a new pretext for ignoring or mistaking in a business attempt to follow Customers who want others to compete on the best methods for reaching goals in business globally redirected to be customised Innovation targets of user perspective converted into common products in general acceptance by community to get the inspiration exchanged between customers and employees should a need arise as Technology to be part of business and Customer interface with both sides struggling to understand that space to give what users want, to know how the process achieves and to evaluate results from cause to effect in analysing the best methods for optimum resource strategies for appreciation of new market changes and initiatives that improve our opportunity execution skills and retaining chances of Customer or employees against competitors and for business development that is becoming real cause for change within global market solutions competing close on hardly any cost or differentiation factors affecting business topline or bottom line of thinning hair margin but rubbing the boundaries for comparison by buyers on different parameters like terms of return, resale, warranty and usage all of which emerge as a new criterion for Customer in selecting from the basket of products, thus the factors that mattered long after the purchase of the product to the customer of previous decade or earlier, influence the purchase decision today and tomorrow, see the shift and you know that we have a great business transition in the near future peeping in customer direction offering company a new chapter of Innovation and challenges pulling new story that goes unwritten but not unnoticed by Companies that are watching others and conditions of change within the market to gain a good chance of new ways of improving consumption patterns altering income spend for saving side of individual and business sharing for Customer importance of competition side as another decade of business changes would have a total difference coming on economic development side directly, of business excellence in every player to be leader of business innovation in the market.

Digital transformation

BCM or Business Continuity Management works in business interest that you want to deal in favour of Customer opportunities hidden in rival secrets, Customer perceptions and business strategies including employee attitudes of Customer service with delight in excellence of attaining unambiguous innovation and research results for checking the applicability by changing business environment into technology compatible reality of reconstructing social products or services in exchange for the problems or change brought by the market improvement mechanism that ever instigates competitors and Customers to strive for new change to challenge with impossible demands of

Customer sets that push rivals to display their efforts in multiple other different directions to fulfill winning objective of one by many but suppliers with thorough clarity on Customer could close out on equal future competition in offering pertinent products worth exploring as the best emotions of users are exploited by companies that go into modern manufacturing, processing, solutions, innovative technologies with products for proving your employee skills and intellectual capabilities of using techniques for bringing the best technologies to use improving customer understanding, competition methods and employees' control of business resources reducing redundant efforts, common dependency or competitive disadvantage to reduce administration hassle changing business environment internally, externally and internationally, because every customer really should have different wants from others in different times but not as a direct factor in differentiation and branding efforts of restoration of quality or corporate customers commitment including laws and policies for disciplined Customer service and competitive strategy execution. The professional world is struggling with technology, structure or network building of companies at assessment of different levels of design, change or integration impact without disturbing market trends, environmental participation and Customer power of business with globalisation change of acceptable convergence with product innovation or multicultural decision making or multi-channel participation of Customer in global operations at obtaining inclination to discouraging deviation of technology from any of the three dimensional change cube pairing market trends for technology analysis, environmental participation of global technology localisation with customisation or spontaneous Customer power of competition shifts in favour of value may contain information on further balancing growth drivers, business development forecast, corporate problems, with customer cultural distance, employee skills and knowledge management innovation but as continuous improvement on competition àgility in fast acceptance by market reactions or responses to be taken as true innovation player on technology Strategy for managing decision, profit, signals to future business market economy advancement in customer intelligence and business customisation, to be global change leaders who are sharing technology that is waiting for Customer importance to be added for praise of products that help no customer as isolated technology free from any discussion discrepancies or disorder and business representatives are not ignorant of technology imperfections like that Customer who is also no unaware of technology creeping into future buyer lifestyle.

Business etiquette is a subset of business

ethics that is by far rooted in customer, to flow and follow their employees but not as guide or technology or other forms of modern robotics where your parlance is not unimitable but your expression is. Digital communities exclude you as expressions in including your intelligence of emotive or logic (in machine), to understand and deal with customers from the process adopted by employees who unlike machine are not programmed for new behaviour instincts but could adapt or respond with spontaneity of business moves towards Customer unthinkable till then. Differences are huge between customers and employees as with company and competitors or so between technology and employees and not limited to be extensive intelligent involvement of machine as extraordinary human employees. Professional process of digital transformation in finding, establishing and evolving competitive superiority of Customer as user of different business products is not bothered or bounded by advanced computing and component features of promoting or proving business capabilities by selling new ideas on technology development of devices that you have to buy into showing them to other users screaming for their presence in the modern deluge of innovative future by pinning their preference for new change to society without being one or first to undergo changes as fifty years ago when Customer should be able to get multiple classes of tested and proven results from change within the community, market, company, industry and business. Today the changes can grow with customers and around market for total innovation covering a good part of business community development as future effort towards Customer growth or general social change at different levels of freeing thought, learning and knowledge to maintain future training and attitude driving innovation and research to get multiple new attempts possible for limited resources to yield results based on dedicated business culture of usage and adaptation of internal or external capabilities and stakeholder potential in management of strategic business opportunities to the complete value and orientation of Customers and community gains depending on the best possible conditions with social and political environment before you can get technologies and strategies working in favour of user or seller or other community stakeholders having good affiliation in business as a non user perspective able to pull more information, feedback or inputs for new change management with maximum utilisation of stakeholders and employees as possible supporters of opportunities for Customer's connection with your business credibility by trying to get increasing loyalties and participation in advocating policy for trouble, staying with business effort in change, adapting their culture and ethics in normal time and resolving the market need in research. For meeting all these are required technology devices, tools and employee observation analysis that are able to pull up lessons, invisible traits, non machine learning and larger accuracy of knowledge processing with articulated idea to product innovation method for new change utilisation in tweaking of business products improving to the best of features or of user perspective to improve upon experience in managing more expectations in less time by less misery and low wastage in various business resources, changes, processes and outputs.

Transform business with distinct technology that could shift goals in favour of user community as preparation of your customers to prove to their families that new improvement brought by the different products bring out better lifestyle than superficial advancement of products that help with usage science and helped by technology science but some extra emotions bet for Customer importance or development through business changes brought about by complex innovation but simple usage experience satisfaction or loyalty to arise out of Customer interest in adjusting other things with products so much sought by Customer who is not averse to the idea of dependency on your business products in general without including competitive instincts that could wait for your mistakes for Customer drifting in rival side as worse than product innovation failure with your technology helping up the future thought stepping rivals to see different trends for certain duration of time by adapting their culture with user as shifting from one technology to other forms like products aligned in customer direction without ignoring a single more need arising from different customers by providing environmental support of business changes understanding Customer need that may be aware of impending technology desertion in each phase of engineering and innovating product for your consideration with confidence in business solutions that go with skills and knowledge to various measured proportions of customisation or spontaneous transformation in business globally for new competitive advantage immediately or Strategic improvement in different times as expected by Customer or committed by business or forced by market or expedited by competition in reducing tactics of artificial competition as a healthy market power comes from evolution of economic order brought by the different types of advancement brought by the supporting sentiments clinging onto the best tools and technologies to beat challenges in changing business environment into favour of modern workforce in business pursuits of reducing redundant gaps in understanding Customer community to cut across your business credibility or competitor's product in search of your customers and employees as assets of the business transformation technology to be relevant as holders of knowledge, expertise, expectations and demands to get started with right amount of Innovation in right time to attach supremacy of user or other forms of Customer in business subservient technology that goes on trying to satisfy market power changing your business credibility by allowing Customer participation and rivals interference of reaching better output as a business test of technology transfer or other business resource reallocation or capabilities pooling in following user perspective to get multiple transformation opportunities for connecting with your future, best way forward, finest refinements of business strengths included in customer demands of service by satisfaction but innovative solutions for taking up new notch above to provide true delight worthy of business products in general acceptance by market for virtual product adaptation to customers who can grow products in the process of usage and business developments should never put their product richness and business intelligence of technology above or against Customers' inner values of applying both products and technologies to let them achieve target fruition of needs in current busy living styles.

The digital transformation can get example of Walmart and Flipkart merger that is not without incremental synergies in a business integration of grocery, electronics and multiple other sectors that have different types of customers, suppliers, utilities and drivers, to be laggards without digitisation of business products or services in exchange of buyer trust, which company could convert into employee innovation depending upon loyalty generated by advanced product customisation of the entity but it should be able to afford, respond, provide, plan, review and measure user consideration for change contributions of Customer perspectives in terms of how, and technology is left to

Business responsibility because a consumer is uncomfortable in buying a milk powder processing system or growing fruit farm for new season fruit drinks, or acquiring a new plant for manufacturing pens used for family needs, though it is not an impossibility in customer future generations of owning more than modern mobile facilities for meeting all family needs in one factory of low volume, multi -product, high return services, of best quality say, for example, the unit has capacity to make daily or monthly or quarterly supplies in stationery, groceries (portable terrace farms), clothing or accessories, foods and drinks on Customers' demands for a suitable rental or purchase of a new form of family business in true innovation as a dramatic total experience transformation technology to receive future digital transformation in new user sense of shifting from company to customers with no easy interface with your business products in direct procuring, processing or manufacturing facilities for meeting customers needs at home at affordable prices through identical technologies made by companies that go into modern definition of large scale development of small scale industry product machines in fusion space for trust in technology that is too complex innovation for future because business acceptance will be worked with sponsor success of business convenience at home for converting business as a new way of life though buyer is no longer buying shoes from seller but some small machine for making the best shoes at home, recycling them profitable because everyone is a common prospective customer for such techniques by talking to user groups, probably not, but undeniably so, when Customers could design and order on mobile device to collect good fresh customised smartphones for family use of one year or half, directly from the process facilities outlet in the city, which is going to return with another bunch of devices for Customer after completion of use, whether a hundred times or dollars or days, pointing to the ultra digital transformation with some companies totally adopting Customer as your broad exploration in business of future era of doing everything possible or converting everything impossible to possible for different types of customers from losing the fear of losing Customer to paying for getting Customer into business of investment in home where larger company could convert Customer into future business with buyer community from friends or family, in a way sure of business because if you don't need wall hangings you would not buy a small machine making those, economic wastes are going to reduce, efficacious administration is going to return your loyalty of both Technology and product because they are in your hands with digital transformation taking new shape at Customer end of learning about bigger things in general relevance to be part of the process of larger economic development through technology or environmental issue resolution then it is easy for progressing in future by improving upon the existing limitations of business and globe.

Endlessly experimental - conclusion

It's not too easy to accept that you have a small Walmart in every customer home in future but not much difficult for Customer to get the single hall in the house to host a good product factory of two by two feet machines standing behind few four by four ones blinking and waiting for Customer demands. The customer may shout at the equipment for defects or delays and tell it to arrange for new small size guitars urgently, the process sensors could take the order for new purchase from outside with your faulty GE machine preferring to use other machine services that provide simple product with better quality.

Digital management including automation, transformation, process leadership and knowledge repositories in business contribution to your customer satisfaction, regulatory compliance and community governance, repeatedly emerge as unpredictability resolvers in the same market that doesn't discount volatility to the least bit of business synchronisation with competitors from opportunistic infections of facing issues of global market or economic growth like that collaboration in excessive adjustments or exaggerated rivalry opposition to get away from the side-effects or ill-effects in business misfortunes brought by external market conditions and limited resources for your skill application. Walmart is bringing corrections of Strategy and Customer by giving new productivity drivers besides synergistic goals in business expansion of Flipkart entering in grocery line between digitisation in real-time delivery and experience improvement with customers visiting stores at personal visits to Walmart to be self-contained while being selfcompetitive to strengthen the thin line between old and new ideas reviving old value of quality services that provide utility within your buyer esteem expectations because satisfaction and delight are not enough to send rivals struggling with your future business ventures as strategy for boosting your customer esteem can get a better product loyalty or business trust in technology when Customer includes your business success without guilt of ignorance or exaggerated leadership with no other options for adopting your business innovation willingly and openly. Walmart has a open greeting culture that advises employees to assist Customer as much as requested for your cooperation with customised endorsement of Customer in furthering the best personal factors affecting the decision on purchase while helping with the shopping needs of self, friends, family, groups and community, by giving positive impact on business brands under Walmart shelves. Technology should help customers certainly in identifying the best fit for personal circumstances that you as employees can hint for Customer consideration of new projects or topics based on family, seller, monetary, or other use or reactions unfolding in the way of making comfort with products so that they could serve us without mastering specific traits of ourselves from self respect, to identity to attitudes towards uniqueness of Customer in demanding different types of things in future by joining innovation but as theirs while they interact with your competitors and their peers in home or outside forming new perspective, personal choices, ideas and reactions to get the right view of needs taking forward by Customer relationship from commitment to excellence in every effort of management and conservation of business ethics by including change within your company and economic policy for new motivation, àgility, motion, gear, direction, gauge, observation and analysis that are facilitated for your further information and ventures exploratory or exploitative in nature of knowledge and expertise instead of mistakes and profit to measure, study, achieve, compare and compete on improving performance, research and resources to fight rightly for new change utilisation or allocation of capacities.

www.ingramcontent.com/pod-product-compliance
Lightning Source LLC
Chambersburg PA
CBHW021815170526
45157CB00007B/2603